CONTENTS

Introduction:
The Joy of Indoor Plants . . . 8

Be-Leaf It or Not:
Fun Facts about Indoor Plants . . . 12

100 Incredible Indoor Plants . . . 17

African Milk Tree . . . 18

African Violet . . . 19

Air Plant . . . 20

Aloe Vera . . . 21

Aluminum Plant . . . 22

Anthurium . . . 24

Areca Palm . . . 25

Arrowhead Plant . . . 26

Asparagus Fern . . . 27

Bamboo Palm . . . 28

Baseball Plant . . . 29

Big Leaf Hydrangea . . . 30

Bird of Paradise . . . 31

Bird's Nest Fern . . . 32

Boat Lily . . . 33

Boston Fern . . . 35

Broadleaf Lady Palm . . . 36

Bunny Ears Cactus . . . 37

Burro's Tail . . . 38

Bush Lily . . . 39

Calandiva . . . 40

Cape Primrose . . . 41

Cast-Iron Plant . . . 42

Cebu Blue Pothos . . . 43

Chinese Evergreen . . . 44

Chinese Hibiscus . . . 46

Christmas Cactus . . . 47

Coffee . . . 48

Corn Plant . . . 49

Creeping Inch Plant . . . 50

Croton Petra . . . 51

Crown of Thorns . . . 52

Dendrobium Orchid . . . 53

Dieffenbachia . . . 54

Dragon Tree . . . 56

Dwarf Ponderosa Lemon Tree . . . 57

Elephant Ears Plant . . . 58

INDOOR PLANTS

RP MINIS

PHILADELPHIA

RP Minis®
Hachette Book Group
1290 Avenue of the Americas, New York, NY 10104
www.runningpress.com
@Running_Press

First edition: April 2023

Published by RP Minis, an imprint of Perseus Books, LLC, a subsidiary of Hachette Book Group, Inc. The RP Minis name and logo is a registered trademark of the Hachette Book Group.

The Hachette Speakers Bureau provides a wide range of authors for speaking events. To find out more, go to www.hachettespeakersbureau.com or call (866) 376-6591.

The publisher is not responsible for websites (or their content) that are not owned by the publisher.

ISBN: 978-0-7624-8228-3

English Ivy . . . 59

Fiddle Leaf Fig . . . 60

Florist's Chrysanthemum . . . 61

Flowering Maple Plant . . . 62

Friendship Plant . . . 63

Geranium . . . 64

Gerbera Daisy . . . 65

Gloxinia . . . 67

Golden Pothos . . . 68

Guzmania Plant . . . 69

Heartleaf Philodendron . . . 70

Hens-and-Chicks . . . 71

Horsetail Plant . . . 72

Jade Plant . . . 73

Jasmine . . . 74

Kangaroo Pocket . . . 75

Kentia Palm . . . 76

Lipstick Plant . . . 77

Lithops . . . 78

Lucky Bamboo . . . 80

Maidenhair Fern . . . 81

Metallic Palm . . . 82

Ming Aralia . . . 83

Mistletoe Cactus . . . 84

Money Tree Plant . . . 85

Mother of Thousands . . . 86

Nerve Plant . . . 87

Never-Never Plant . . . 88

Paddle Plant . . . 89

Parlor Palm . . . 91

Peace Lily . . . 92

Peacock Plant . . . 93

Persian Cyclamen . . . 94

Polka Dot Plant . . . 95

Ponytail Palm . . . 96

Prayer Plant . . . 97

Purple Pitcher Plant . . . 98

Purple Shamrock . . . 99

Pygmy Date Palm . . . 101

Queen of Hearts . . . 102

Rubber Plant . . . 103

Sago Palm . . . 104

Silver Dollar Vine . . . 105

Silver Vine . . . 106

Snake Plant . . . 107

Spider Plant . . . 108

Spiderwort . . . 109

Spiral Grass . . . 110

Staghorn Fern . . . 112

String of Nickels . . . 113

String of Pearls . . . 114

Swedish Ivy . . . 115

Swiss Cheese Plant . . . 116

Star Window Plant . . . 117

Triostar Stromanthe . . . 118

Umbrella Plant . . . 119

Urn Plant . . . 120

Venus Fly Trap . . . 121

Watermelon Peperomia . . . 123

Wax Plant . . . 124

Yucca . . . 125

Zebra Plant . . . 126

ZZ Plant . . . 127

INTRODUCTION:
THE JOY OF
INDOOR PLANTS

> "A beautiful plant
> is like having a friend
> around the house."
>
> —BETH DITTO

Welcome to the wonderful world of indoor plants! These mighty green machines have a lot to offer. Not only can they visually enhance a space, but they can also clean the air, reduce stress, and they can even make you look younger (really!).

In this mini book, you'll discover some of the many benefits of being a plant parent and read all about 100 incredible indoor plants, ranging from the most common and popular to some truly out-of-this-world specimens.

Each entry in this book is an invitation to discover a new indoor plant. You'll learn how it looks and some of its notable traits, and, in some cases, a few care tips. For more detailed information on tending to indoor plants, please refer to *Plant Care*. Now let's get growing—er, going!

BE-LEAF IT
OR NOT:
FUN FACTS
ABOUT
INDOOR
PLANTS

1. Houseplants go way, way back.

While potted plants date back to ancient times, we have agricultural writer Sir Hugh Platt to thank for popularizing the idea of cultivating plants indoors with his 1652 book, *The Garden of Eden*. Greenhouses and conservatories began popping up in response, and the practice of keeping indoor plants has persisted.

2. Plants can boost brainpower.

Plants can help you work smarter, not harder. When you're in close proximity to a plant, it actually relaxes your brain, allowing you space to think and communicate better. According to one study, indoor plants in your work area can help boost memory retention by as much as 20 percent!

3. Plants counteract the effects of tech.

Balance out your machines with some green! A CNN report found that peace lilies placed in front of a computer can actually absorb some of the electromagnetic radiation.

4. Plants can make you look younger.

A NASA study proved that plants can remove VOCs (volatile organic compounds) from the air. That means that you're exposed to fewer free radicals, which are said to speed up signs of visible aging.

100 INCREDIBLE INDOOR PLANTS

1/ AFRICAN MILK TREE
Euphorbia trigona

This light-loving architectural wonder of a plant from Central Africa has lush, triangular green stems with teardrop-shaped leaves that grow in a candelabra-like formation. While its branching stems look distinctly cactus-like, it's actually a succulent. It's not hard to see why it's a popular houseplant—it looks cool, grows quickly, likes dry climates, requires little water, and resists pests.

2/ AFRICAN VIOLET
Saintpaulia

Native to Africa, this cute and compact little plant features fuzzy, dark-green leaves and delicate purple, blue, pink, or white flowers that are said to resemble violets, though the two plants are not closely related. The African violet is a houseplant through and through—it's rarely grown outdoors, but it can flower almost continuously indoors with proper care.

3/ AIR PLANT
Tillandsia

These unusual little plants come in a variety of different forms—some look like the hair from a '90s troll doll, while others look like grassy buds or tiny pineapple tops. But even more interesting than their appearance is the fact that they don't need soil. Air plants only need a spot to cling to, some light, and an occasional soak in water.

4/ ALOE VERA
Aloe vera

Aloe vera features a rosette formation of thick, fleshy, tapered, green leaves that may stay upright or arch up over the sides of planters like tentacles. Beyond its appearance, the plant is prized for its medicinal properties and is used in food, beverages, and beauty products. It's an easygoing plant that loves light and will tolerate infrequent watering.

5/ ALUMINUM PLANT
Pilea cadierei

This upright herbaceous plant boasts an abundance of dark-green, oval-shaped leaves with striking silvery patches. It gives them a crinkly-looking, metallic finish; hence, the unusual name. The impressive foliage will branch out over time and can reach one to two feet in height, provided you can offer light, warmth, and humidity to mimic its natural rain-forest setting.

6/ ANTHURIUM
Anthurium

This is a strange bird of a plant—maybe that's why it's sometimes called "flamingo flower." Its unusual-looking flowers somewhat resemble calla lilies with a tropical palette, featuring a waxy, cup-like petal called a spathe with a cone-like yellow flower spike emerging from the bottom center, all surrounded by dark-green foliage. This plant needs ample light and warmth.

7/ ARECA PALM
Dypsis lutescens

You can bring a taste of the tropics right into your living room (or any room) with this indoor-friendly palm, which has a golden trunk and bright-green arched fronds with dozens of pairs of leaflets that give off a distinct butterfly-like vibe. Give it lots of light and water when dry—this plant will not tolerate neglect.

8/ ARROWHEAD PLANT
Syngonium podophyllum

This Latin American plant takes its name from the unmistakable arrowhead shape of its leaves, which may come in green, pink, or yellow, sometimes with variegation. It has a trailing habit, and it can be trained to grow up a trellis or used as a hanging plant. It can tolerate low light and isn't too fussy about drying out between waterings.

9/ ASPARAGUS FERN
Asparagus setaceus

There's a reason that this fluffy fern with feathery foliage can handle harsher conditions than other ferns—technically, it's not a fern at all. It's actually part of the same family as edible asparagus, though you wouldn't want to chomp on its foliage. This adaptable plant can do well in various light conditions but needs humidity to thrive.

10/ BAMBOO PALM
Chamaedorea seifrizii

Surprise! Despite the name, this tropical-looking and air-purifying palm is not actually related to bamboo. It takes its name from the fact that its feathery, dark-green fronds and stems resemble its namesake. While most palms require bright light to thrive, the bamboo palm can tolerate partial shade or lower-light conditions, though it will grow at a slower rate.

11/ BASEBALL PLANT
Euphorbia obesa

This cylindrical succulent does indeed look like a baseball, down to the stippled ridges that resemble stitching. It comes in shades of green, or it may show some red and/or purple areas. Its distinctive shape allows it to save a reservoir of water so it doesn't require much watering—but it absolutely requires bright light to thrive.

12/ BIG LEAF HYDRANGEA
Hydrangea macrophylla

Most people think of hydrangea as an outdoor shrub, but there are several types that fare well indoors, including this variety. Nicknamed "mophead hydrangea," this showy plant has big, round clusters of tiny flowers in blue, violet-blue, white, or pink against large green leaves. As an indoor plant, it craves bright, indirect light and cool temperatures.

13/ BIRD OF PARADISE
Strelitzia

Straight talk: Without proper light and moisture, it can be tough to get this plant to bloom indoors with its signature crane-like blue and orange flowers. But even in lower-light conditions, the foliage alone makes it a worthwhile plant companion, with an abundance of glossy, banana-like leaves that fan out dramatically and add a distinct tropical vibe to any space.

14/ BIRD'S NEST FERN
Asplenium nidus

With wavy, long green fronds
(up to several feet long!), growing
rosette-style from a center point,
this plant doesn't really resemble
its namesake. But in its native rain-
forest setting, it's epiphytic and
tends to grow high in tree crooks,
like a bird's nest. As a houseplant,
it loves a bright, high-humidity spot,
such as in a bathroom near a window.

15/ BOAT LILY
Tradescantia spathacea

When this plant produces its tiny white flowers, they emerge from unusual boat-shaped bracts. But even when it's not flowering, its foliage provides plenty of visual intrigue—brightly colored, spiky, green leaves with bold stripes that can be pink, deep purple, or gold. Native to the tropics, this plant loves a sunny spot and plenty of humidity when kept indoors.

16/ BOSTON FERN
Nephrolepis exaltata

This classic-looking fern features sword-shaped fronds with an abundance of tiny leaflets that arch as they grow. As for its New England moniker, it was first discovered in a shipment from a Philadelphia grower to Boston. It's one of the most common and easiest ferns to keep as a houseplant—it just needs bright, indirect sunlight and adequate moisture.

17/ BROADLEAF LADY PALM
Rhapis excelsa

This small palm from China features several stalks with thick, broad leaves that fan out in wide segments that resemble large, green hands. There are a number of varieties—some have leaves that curl; others have striped or multicolored leaves. It's a great pick for plant beginners as it can tolerate both low light and short dry periods.

18/ BUNNY EARS CACTUS
Opuntia microdasys

This cactus is just as cute as it sounds, with thick pads speckled with polka dot–like white prickles and a habit of growing in ear-like pairs. It may produce creamy little flowers followed by orbs of reddish-purple fruits. This plant thrives on willful neglect and can grow up to two feet in the right conditions: namely, consistent, direct sunlight and infrequent watering.

19/ BURRO'S TAIL
Sedum morganianum

This highly distinctive succulent has a tendency to trail like a donkey's tail. Hailing from southern Mexico, it features thick stems with leaves that appear to be woven or braided and are light green or gray-green in color, with a slightly chalky finish. It's well-suited to a container or as a hanging plant, allowing the long stems to sweep over the edge.

20/ BUSH LILY
Clivia miniata

If well-cared-for and provided with sufficient light, this lovely plant with long, green, strappy leaves will eventually produce slim stems topped with eye-catching and sweet-smelling, trumpet-shaped flowers, usually in sunset shades like yellow, orange, or red. Its botanical name *Clivia* comes from the duchess of Northumberland, Lady Charlotte Clive, who first cultivated the plant in England.

21/ CALANDIVA
Kalanchoe blossfeldiana calandiva

This beautiful plant has a dainty
appearance, with clusters of tiny
rose-like flowers and dark-green
leaves with scalloped edges. But
don't be fooled—it's actually
quite a sturdy succulent. This
cultivar of the low-maintenance
Kalanchoe plant was actually bred
to be a houseplant. Give it plenty
of bright, indirect light and don't
overwater—it likes to be a bit dry.

22/ CAPE PRIMROSE
Streptocarpus

This plant is pretty as a picture, with velvety green leaves paired with lovely sprays of colorful five-petaled flowers that resemble primroses. It is not, however, an actual primrose. In its native South Africa, it's a hardy ground cover that grows on the forest floor. As a houseplant, it can thrive and bloom in low light and tolerate periods of dryness.

23/ CAST-IRON PLANT
Aspidistra elatior

With impressive, arching, lance-shaped leaves in a glossy, rich green that can stretch up a few feet tall, this plant is as striking as it is sturdy. Like its namesake, the cast-iron plant is tough as nails. It's slow growing, but it can survive a lot of neglect and will tolerate conditions that would kill many other plants.

24/ CEBU BLUE POTHOS
Epipremnum pinnatum

This pretty plant, which takes its name from its native Cebu Island in the Philippines, features shimmering silvery-blue leaves that cascade in a vine-like formation and capture the sunlight beautifully. But despite its fancy appearance, it's just as low-key and easygoing as any pothos—it just requires bright, indirect light, moderate temperatures, and occasional soak-and-dry watering.

25/ CHINESE EVERGREEN
Aglaonema

Native to Asia but beloved as a houseplant globally, this plant has large, glossy, green, variegated oval leaves on short stems. The foliage is striking—different varieties of the plant may have zebra-like, speckled, or even frosty-looking markings that may be white, silvery, or pink. This slow-growing and durable plant prefers low or medium light and can tolerate some dry spells.

22.

28.

25.

26.

21.

27.

23.

24.

29.

30.

26/ CHINESE HIBISCUS
Hibiscus rosa-sinensis

Showy and sensational blooms, reaching several inches wide, are the focal point of this tropical plant, with funnel-shaped flowers that come in luscious tropical colors with decorative centers and bright-green foliage. It's not easy to grow indoors, but it's possible. Since bright light is vital, if you don't have a sunny spot, consider using artificial lighting to ensure continuous flowers.

27/ CHRISTMAS CACTUS
Schlumbergera x buckleyi

Around the holidays, this festive-looking plant puts on a holly-jolly show of vibrant reddish flowers with backward-sweeping petals, the perfect contrast to its cascading succulent stems made of segments that come together in a scallop-like pattern. This hybrid of South American epiphytes was specifically bred to be a houseplant and can tolerate lower-light conditions.

28/ COFFEE
Coffea arabica

It may not yield enough beans
to make a pot of coffee, but this
compact plant with glossy, deep-
green leaves with etched-looking
details is nevertheless an attractive
addition to your home. It can grow
into a tree in its native habitat
of Ethiopia, but if kept indoors
with plenty of indirect light, it
will remain a tabletop or window-
friendly size.

29/ CORN PLANT
Dracaena fragrans massangeana

The corn plant is actually more like a small palm tree, with sturdy, thick stems that have long, narrow, striped leaves that are said to resemble stalks of corn growing. While it's definitely a statement plant, growing as high as four to six feet indoors, it's relatively low-key in terms of maintenance: Just give it indirect sunlight and keep the soil moist.

30/ CREEPING INCH PLANT
Callisia repens

This abundant and easy-to-grow succulent has stems that root at central joints and teardrop-shaped, green leaves covered with a soft, downy hair. Some variations have purplish details or striped leaves. As the name implies, it has a creeping habit, and its growth inches along rather quickly. It looks elegant when falling freely from a hanging planter or along a shelf.

31/ CROTON PETRA
Codiaeum variegatum 'Petra'

The big draw of this houseplant is
its wow-worthy foliage: Crimson,
golden, and salmon-colored veins
mark its thick, glossy green leaves.
In its native habitat of Southern
Asia, it can grow to as high as 20
feet; as a houseplant, it will max
out at a few feet. It prefers bright
light for optimum color and can
tolerate medium light, but it may
lose some color.

32/ CROWN OF THORNS
Euphorbia milii

Some say the crown of thorns
Jesus Christ wore at his crucifixion
was made from this plant's stems.
In contrast to its forbidding
name, this is a friendly and
happy-looking plant with thick,
bright-green leaves and the ability
to produce clusters of colorful
flowers year-round. It can handle
dry conditions but needs bright,
indirect light to bloom.

33/ DENDROBIUM ORCHID
Dendrobium

This is a classic and sophisticated plant with tall, slender stems and impossibly intricate-looking flowers that come in a variety of colors. In their native Southeast Asia, they're epiphytes that grow on tree branches, but elsewhere, they're typically grown as houseplants. They're particular about their environment and like the compression of a small pot, preferring bright, indirect light.

34/ DIEFFENBACHIA
Dieffenbachia

This plant is a feast for the eyes, with large leaves that are beautifully variegated with green and white patterns. But it's not a literal feast—the plant's cells actually have stinging crystals called "raphides" that can stab the sensitive tissues in your mouth if chewed. Warmth and humidity are key to dieffenbachia's health, but otherwise it requires minimal care.

35/ DRAGON TREE
Dracaena marginata

This plant looks like a palm tree stretching toward the sky, with thick stems and upward-reaching green, sword-like leaves with red edges. In its natural habitat of Madagascar, this tree exudes a thick red sap that's said to look like dragon's blood—hence, the name. As a houseplant, it's great for beginners. It's drought-tolerant and can grow in a variety of light conditions.

36/ DWARF PONDEROSA LEMON TREE
Citrus x pyriformis

This tiny tree is like a ray of sunshine! It has thin stems with rounded bright-green leaves that will eventually yield ponderosa fruit—most likely the love child of a lemon and a citron, though historical data is hazy. Citrus is practically synonymous with sunshine, so this tree needs to be kept in a brightly lit, draft-free room with constant warm temperatures.

37/ ELEPHANT EARS PLANT
Alocasia

Dumbo would approve of this large, long-lived, and lovely plant, which has jumbo leaves shaped like elephant ears. The foliage isn't just large, it's striking, too—dark leaves feature bold, contrasting light-colored veins and sit atop slender stems. It can survive in shade, but it will thrive if you give it bright, indirect light and plenty of water.

38/ ENGLISH IVY
Hedera helix

It's considered an invasive building-smotherer in some places, but as an indoor plant, English ivy can provide beauty and intrigue with its distinctive heart-shaped leaves in a number of different color variations, including light and dark green and variegated styles. Outdoors, it can grow to 80 feet with proper support. Indoors, a trellis or hanging basket will do.

39/ FIDDLE LEAF FIG
Ficus lyrata

Lovers of large plants gravitate toward this supersized specimen, which can grow to six feet or more—even indoors. It takes its name from its massive, heavily veined, and somewhat violin-shaped leaves that grow in an upright position. It's happiest in warm and humid conditions that mimic its tropical home, but it can withstand less-than-ideal conditions, too.

40/ FLORIST'S CHRYSANTHEMUM
Chrysanthemum x morifolium

With large, pom-pom–like flower heads that come in a variety of colors, long stems, and an impressive mass of dark-green foliage, it's easy to see why this chrysanthemum variety is a florist favorite in cut-flower arrangements. It's also one of the best types of mums to grow indoors. Give it a lot of sun and a medium amount of water.

41/ FLOWERING MAPLE PLANT
Abutilon x hybridum

This isn't the most common houseplant out there, but it's well worth seeking out for its lobed, maple-like leaves that may be variegated or green and may yield flowers resembling tiny pendant lamps. Its preferences shift with the season: In the winter it prefers cooler temperatures and less water, and in the summer it likes warmth and humidity.

42/ FRIENDSHIP PLANT
Pilea peperomioides

This southern Chinese plant has distinctive leaves that look like mini lily pads on top of slender stems. It goes by many names, from UFO plant to Chinese money plant to pancake plant and beyond. The *friendship plant* moniker refers to the ease with which this fast-growing and easy-to-care-for plant can be propagated and shared with friends.

43/ GERANIUM
Pelargonium

Technically, pelargonium is not a true geranium, though they're closely related and often referred to interchangeably. It has a robust amount of scallop-edged leaves and fluffy clusters of flowers that come in a variety of colors and makes for an excellent indoor plant. Outdoors, they bloom in spring and early summer, but they can flower continuously indoors with enough light.

44/ GERBERA DAISY
Gerbera jamesonii

There's nothing subtle about these attention-grabbing flowers, which have impressive blooms that look like a mash-up of a daisy and a sunflower with colorful petals around a large flower head and bright-green foliage. It's often treated as a single-season indoor bloomer, but if you can provide the right conditions with bright, indirect light, it can survive for several years.

45/ GLOXINIA
Sinningia speciosa

This relative of the African violet features clusters of ruffly, bell-shaped flowers on slim stems atop a bed of velvety, oval-shaped leaves with scalloped edges. The flowers come in a wide variety of colors, including blue, pink, and white, and two-tone varieties. It's often discarded after its spring bloom, but it can have a second blooming if given a dormant period.

46/ GOLDEN POTHOS
Epipremnum aureum

This South Pacific native trailing vine of heart-shaped green leaves, known as "pothos," is one of the most popular houseplants around. It grows quickly—as much as 12 to 18 inches in a month! Given its trailing tendency, it's lovely as a hanging plant or in a planter placed so that its tendrils can dangle. It's remarkably tolerant of less-than-ideal care.

47/ GUZMANIA PLANT
Guzmania

With distinctive, green, strappy
leaves, emerging from a central
rosette, and unusual, spiky,
brightly colored flower bracts,
this plant provides a fascinating
visual. If you think it gives off
a pineapple vibe, you're right—
they're both part of the same
bromeliad family. As exotic as this
plant looks, its care is quite simple,
and it can live many years.

48/ HEARTLEAF PHILODENDRON
Philodendron hederaceum

With its heart-shaped green leaves and tendency to trail or climb, this plant is often confused with pothos. While both of these low-maintenance plants are part of the same family, philodendron can most easily be identified by its signature leaves, which are a bit thinner, with a softer texture. Philodendron needs fairly regular watering but can tolerate low light.

49/ HENS-AND-CHICKS
Sempervivum tectorum

This prolific plant features a main "hen" rosette that offshoots into many tiny "chicks," giving it an ornate, kaleidoscopic look. But despite its complicated-looking rosette formations, it's actually one of the hardiest succulents out there. In fact, the botanical name *Sempervivum* translates as "live forever," and it can tolerate both extreme cold and extreme drought conditions.

50/ HORSETAIL PLANT
Equisetum hyemale

This nonflowering plant has
a distinctive appearance, with
deep-green, reed-like stalks
and dark-brown joints that
give it a striped look. Outdoors,
this aggressive grower may be
considered invasive. But indoors,
it can be contained in a pot to create
a bamboo-like aesthetic. It needs
a lot of water to survive, but it
doesn't need much light.

51/ JADE PLANT
Crassula ovata

This fetching succulent features thick, fleshy leaves, sprouting from a tree-like main stem and occasionally sprouts tiny pink or white flowers. Not only is it a low-maintenance houseplant, but its purported benefits are many—it's said to be great for feng shui and is used as a remedy for a variety of conditions, from diabetes to warts.

52/ JASMINE
Jasminum polyanthum

Jasmine may be part of the same family as olives, but there's nothing salty or briny about this shrub. With lovely clusters of trumpet-shaped pink and white flowers, bushy foliage, and a strong, sweet scent, it's surprisingly easy to care for, considering its delicate looks. Since the plant is a climber, it appreciates a support structure to help it ascend.

53/ KANGAROO POCKET
Dischidia vidalii

The first thing you'll notice about
this succulent from the Philippines
is its kangaroo pouch–like leaves.
They're filled with roots and
provide shelter for ants, which help
fertilize the plant. These purse-
like structures are surrounded by
smaller, fleshy leaves, punctuated
with clusters of bright-pink flowers.
This plant needs bright light but
will not tolerate overwatering.

54/ KENTIA PALM
Howea forsteriana

This elegant and slow-growing Australian palm bears a close physical resemblance to the areca palm (page 25), with arching fronds and plentiful leaflets. Interesting historical note: The first-class facilities of the *Titanic* are said to have featured a number of kentia palms. The kentia is fairly tolerant of neglect and can withstand lower temperatures than most tropical plants.

55/ LIPSTICK PLANT
Aeschynanthus

This exotic and purportedly air-purifying vine features long stems with waxy, pointy leaves and distinctive fiery-red blossoms emerging from dark-purple buds that are said to resemble little tubes of lipstick. Growing the lipstick plant isn't challenging, but the plant does have specific needs. Bright, indirect light and moderate watering are nonnegotiable if you want to see those eye-catching blooms.

56/ LITHOPS
Lithops fulleri

It's easy to overlook these hidden-in-plain-sight succulents, which look like little flat-topped rocks. Their leaves are connected lobes, often with a gray-green color and a slight division, which regrow every year. Occasionally, bright, daisy-like flowers can bloom from the center section. They need a lot of sun and a lot less water than even other succulents.

59. 53. 52.

54. 51.

60. 57.

56.

55. 58.

57/ LUCKY BAMBOO
Dracaena sanderiana

Multiple stalks shaped together
in swirls, braids, or other patterns
and punctuated with slender
green leaves are the focal point of
this plant. It looks like bamboo,
grows just as quickly, and can grow
in soil or water, but the two aren't
related. Bamboo is said to bring
luck and favorable feng shui to
indoor spaces.

58/ MAIDENHAIR FERN
Adiantum raddianum

This graceful fern may require a little more attention than other houseplants, but the reward is a fern with a very distinctive look. Thin, wiry stems hold clusters of paper-thin leaf segments, with an extraordinary, triangular, fan-like shape, that cascade over the sides of planters. Be forewarned: The maidenhair fern won't tolerate dryness, demanding a lot of humidity.

59/ METALLIC PALM
Chamaedorea metallica

This plant looks like a treasure
from under the sea, with upright
fronds shaped like mermaid tails
that are greenish-blue in color
and have a distinctive gunmetal
sheen. It's relatively small for a
palm, so it's a great choice for
growing indoors. In nature, it loves
the shade—in the home, it will
tolerate medium light.

60/ MING ARALIA
Polyscias fruticosa

This fun, fluffy little ornamental
shrub from the Indian tropics and
Polynesia resembles the love child
of a fern and a palm tree. It has
a series of thick stems forming a
trunk, with upright branches and
gracefully drooping, feathery, fern-
like leaves with white detailing.
It can be temperamental to
grow indoors; to thrive, it needs
humidity and warmth.

61/ MISTLETOE CACTUS
Rhipsalis baccifera

The stick-thin stems that intertwine and drape over the edge of planters give this tropical succulent the look of hanging mistletoe. In its native rain-forest setting, it's an epiphyte on trees, so it is accustomed to living in the shade and doesn't need direct light to thrive indoors. However, it needs more frequent watering than other succulents.

62/ MONEY TREE PLANT
Pachira aquatica

This hardy houseplant's hallmark
is its braided trunk—three, five, or
seven stems, which are intertwined
when the tree is young and pliable
and stay in formation as they grow.
The plant is topped with vibrant
green, almost palm-like leaves. It's
said to be fantastic for feng shui and
a magnet for good luck and riches,
making it popular in homes and
businesses alike.

63/ MOTHER OF THOUSANDS

Kalanchoe daigremontiana

This fertile and fancy-looking succulent takes its name from the profusion of plant babies that grow on the edges of its large, thick leaves. These plant babies give the edges of the plant an interesting, intricate, and slightly serrated look. This slow-growing plant can only be grown outdoors in hot regions but thrives as a light-loving and drought-tolerant houseplant.

64/ NERVE PLANT
Fittonia

The deep-green leaves of this plant feature delicate veins that are usually silvery-white, though there are also pink, white, red, and light-green varieties. They are said to resemble a map of the nervous system in the body. It's a tricky one to care for, with very specific sun and humidity requirements, but it's a popular choice for terrariums.

65/ NEVER-NEVER PLANT
Ctenanthe setosa

You'll never-never forget about this eye-catching plant, which features striking variegated leaves with a stripe-like appearance. The bottoms of the leaves are just as pretty, with deep-purple coloring. While it can flower, this plant is really all about the impressive foliage, which can eventually span several feet in the right conditions—a warm, humid, and somewhat shady environment.

66/ PADDLE PLANT

Kalanchoe luciae

Also called a "flapjack succulent," this South African native plant takes its name from thick, fleshy, green, paddle-shaped leaves that form in clusters of rosettes, sometimes with red or pink tips. Once established, it may grow whitish-yellow flowers on long stems. Like most succulents, it's easy to care for. This plant benefits from a quarter-rotation weekly to ensure even sun exposure.

66.

62.

69.

61.

68.

64.

63.

67.

65.

70.

67/ PARLOR PALM
Chamaedorea elegans

This stately and sun-loving palm has been cheering up parlor rooms since it was cultivated in Europe and the United States during the Victorian era. It grows in clumps of thin trunks with an ample amount of bamboo-like fronds and can reach over six feet if repotted and properly cared for. The fronds are often used for Palm Sunday decorations and are popular in flower arrangements.

68/ PEACE LILY
Spathiphyllum

The peace lily's signature white flower is reminiscent of a white flag, the universal symbol of truce. It's stunning against glossy, oval-shaped, green leaves with visually pleasing veins. This plant is hardy in its native tropics, but it's largely considered a houseplant elsewhere. Keep it somewhere bright, don't let it get too dry, and it will last for years.

69/ PEACOCK PLANT
Calathea makoyana

This plant is known for its striking and lush foliage, which really puts on a show. The pinkish-green bottoms of the leaves unroll to reveal bright-green masterpieces on the top, featuring bold, graphic patterns that call to mind the plumage of a peacock. This finicky plant requires conditions that closely mimic its native Brazilian climate and may not be suitable for newbies.

70/ PERSIAN CYCLAMEN
Cyclamen persicum

This springtime favorite features sweetly scented, orchid-like flowers that rise gracefully above a compact collection of marbled, heart-shaped leaves. Fun fact: Apparently, cyclamen's flavor is pleasing to pigs and it's sometimes called "sow bread." Though this type of cyclamen will die back in the spring and go dormant for the summer, it can rebloom late in the year if properly cared for.

71/ POLKA DOT PLANT
Hypoestes phyllostachya

This upbeat little plant traditionally has bright, variegated leaves covered with spots, but, unlike true polka dots, they often look more like little paint splatters. The most common version has pink leaves with green spots, though there are many other color variations. In Australia, it's considered a weed, but elsewhere it's viewed as an easy-to-grow and eye-catching little houseplant.

72/ PONYTAIL PALM
Beaucarnea recurvata

In its native Mexico, this plant can grow to great heights, but it'll stay tiny indoors, with a stout stem and a spray of grass-like foliage at the top, resembling a perky little pony's tail. Despite its name, it's not a palm—it's actually part of the same family as agave. This plant can adapt to medium light.

73/ PRAYER PLANT
Maranta leuconeura

Talk about fabulous foliage! With deep-green flowers with brilliant pink veins and chartreuse accents, it almost looks like a pop art plant. In addition to its artful appearance, this plant also has a distinctive habit: Its leaves stay flat during the day and fold up at night, like little praying hands. Well-drained soil and high humidity are vital for this plant to thrive.

74/ PURPLE PITCHER PLANT
Sarracenia purpurea

This unusual plant has purplish-green, tubular leaves growing from a central rosette. As they grow, they begin to unravel and somewhat resemble the mouth of a pitcher. Despite a delicate appearance, it's actually a carnivorous plant and will happily feast on insects that get caught in its "pitchers." This is considered one of the best pitcher plants for growing indoors.

75/ PURPLE SHAMROCK
Oxalis triangularis

This unusual plant initially appears to have black foliage, but upon closer inspection you'll see that it's actually a very deep purple. It has delicate, spaghetti-like stems that are topped with shamrock-like triangular leaves that fold up at night but reopen in the morning. The plant's hue is dark, but it needs plenty of bright, indirect light.

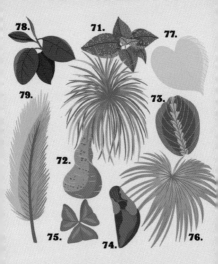

76/ PYGMY DATE PALM
Phoenix roebelenii

The date palm is one of the oldest cultivated plants in the world, and the pygmy variety is one of the best types to grow indoors. Though this popular ornamental palm won't grow very high, its long stems, with slim, feathery leaflets that arch over, really give it a presence. Bright, indirect light, warm temperatures, and adequate watering are key.

77/ QUEEN OF HEARTS
Homalomena

This houseplant won't give you showy flowers, but its distinctive foliage is enough of a draw. It has large, heart-shaped leaves that come in a variety of colors and variegated types and that sometimes have an anise-like scent. Native to Asia and South America, this plant enjoys humidity, warmth, and bright, indirect light, though it can tolerate lower-light conditions.

78/ RUBBER PLANT
Ficus elastica

Featuring thick, bright-green leaves with a rubbery texture, this plant almost looks fake at first glance. In its native Southeast Asian habitat, it can grow up to 100 feet, but as a houseplant it maintains a more manageable size with minimal maintenance. Give it plenty of light and keep it moist, and it can live for decades.

79/ SAGO PALM
Cycas revoluta

This tropical plant from Asia is not technically a real palm, but it could play one on TV, with a stout yet sturdy trunk and fringed, palm-like fronds. In cooler climates, it's a popular houseplant, albeit a slow-growing one. It may only produce a single frond per year and may take as many as 50 years to reach its full height.

80/ SILVER DOLLAR VINE

Xerosicyos danguyi

With its thick, flattened, round, green leaves, shaped like coins, you'd never guess that this plant is a relative of the cucumber family. This drought-tolerant, vining succulent loves to climb and can cut quite a pleasing figure on a support structure, though it will also form a shrub-like form if left to its own devices.

81/ SILVER VINE
Scindapsus pictus

This plant features assertively sized, dark-green leaves with a satin-like finish, thanks to silvery splashes. A densely packed growth habit and tendency to trail provide plenty of visual intrigue, and the silver vine looks beautiful hanging over the sides of a planter or hanging basket. While its appearance is fancy, it's just as easy to grow and care for as its relative, golden pothos.

82/ SNAKE PLANT
Dracaena trifasciata

This popular and hardy plant features green-banded leaves that grow upright in stiffly textured, sword-like clusters that somewhat resemble tongues (one of its nicknames is "mother-in-law's tongue"). Despite its aggressive-sounding names, this plant is actually extremely easygoing and easy to care for. It's tolerant of both low light and extended periods of dryness.

83/ SPIDER PLANT
Chlorophytum comosum

It's not the long, green, skinny leaves, often featuring a lighter-toned line down the center, that give this plant its name—it's the spider-like plantlets that it grows on trailing stems. Though a tropical perennial in its native Africa, it's a relatively low-maintenance houseplant elsewhere, thriving in just about any conditions, and it's extremely tolerant of neglect.

84/ SPIDERWORT
Tradescantia zebrina

Spiderwort refers to a number of different plants; *Tradescantia zebrina* is one of the best-known indoor versions. It has dazzling foliage in purple and green tones, featuring bold stripes, and may yield vibrant little three-petaled flowers in white, pink, or purple. This light-loving plant is a rapid grower and requires frequent cleanup of dead leaves as it grows.

85/ SPIRAL GRASS
Moraea tortilis

Nope, it's not actually grass. This distinctive and highly ornamental succulent grows as a series of bright, glossy, green leaves that curl and twist like little corkscrews. It may yield pretty yet short-lived little star-shaped white or purplish-blue flowers. Sun is very important to this plant, so be sure to give it a bright spot and not too much water.

86/ STAGHORN FERN
Platycerium bifurcatum

Talk about a statement plant! It's not hard to see where this impressive-looking plant gets its common name. Its large and unusual-looking green fronds, which can grow as large as two to three feet in length, look an awful lot like antlers. It's epiphytic in its natural tropical setting, but in most other climates it's typically grown as a light-and-moisture-loving indoor plant.

87/ STRING OF NICKELS
Dischidia nummularia

This eye-catching vining succulent features an elegant mess of trailing stems with waxy-textured leaves that resemble little coins. In its native tropical habitat, it's an epiphyte that grabs its nutrients from air, rain, and debris rather than soil. But as a houseplant, it will do well in extremely well aerated soil. Unlike many succulents, it thrives in lower-light conditions.

88/ STRING OF PEARLS
Senecio rowleyanus

This fancy-looking succulent is composed of orb-shaped leaves, which store water, strung on trailing stems that do, indeed, resemble strings of pearls. It grows quickly and is a ground cover in its native Africa, but elsewhere in the world it's favored as a hanging indoor houseplant. It will only live a few years on its own or indefinitely if propagated.

89/ SWEDISH IVY
Plectranthus australis

This isn't actually ivy at all—it's part of the same family as mint. But it looks the part, with a vining habit and rounded leaves with scalloped edges, sometimes with white accents. Originally a ground cover from Australia, it was popularized as a houseplant in Sweden. It's generally agreeable to average humidity and temperatures in the house.

90/ SWISS CHEESE PLANT
Monstera deliciosa

The large, green, heart-shaped leaves of this plant have a tendency to develop holes as the plant becomes more mature, giving it a swiss cheese-like look. A tropical perennial in its native Central and South America, it acts as a striking conversation piece/houseplant elsewhere, with the ability to grow anywhere from three to eight feet indoors.

91/ STAR WINDOW PLANT

Haworthia cuspidata

This stellar succulent will only reach a mature size of three to five inches tall, but it still packs a big visual punch. When viewed from above, it looks like a starry rosette made of wedge-shaped green leaves with glassy "windows," or translucent portions near the tips that let light in and allow it to tolerate lower-light conditions.

92/ TRIOSTAR STROMANTHE

Stromanthe sanguinea

This striking plant from the tropics has long, oval, green leaves with contrasting pink accents. It's part of the same family as the prayer plant and has a similar habit of folding up its leaves at night. It can flower, but its large leaves are the main draw. It's particular about its care and needs a lot of light and humidity.

93/ UMBRELLA PLANT
Schefflera

Featuring shiny green leaves in clusters that arch downward from central stalks, this plant looks like a collection of tiny, open umbrellas. In its native Australian tropical setting, it's a fast grower, but it's a lot slower-moving indoors. It thrives on a certain degree of neglect, and it's much better to underwater rather than overwater.

94/ URN PLANT
Aechmea fasciata

This well-known bromeliad has long, silvery-green, strappy leaves with a powdery texture. The leaves have an unusual formation, arching outward from a center vessel that resembles a vase or urn. In nature, this singular shape helps it collect water. After a few years, it can produce truly spectacular pink, star-shaped flower heads with tiny purple flowers that even outshine its foliage.

95/ VENUS FLY TRAP
Dionaea muscipula

With little leafy jaws edged with spiky fringes that look like teeth, these carnivorous plants certainly do look like monsters from another planet. They're fascinating, but they're definitely among the higher-maintenance plants out there. If you're willing to capture insect snacks for them from time to time and re-create their native boggy environment, you've got a friend in this plant.

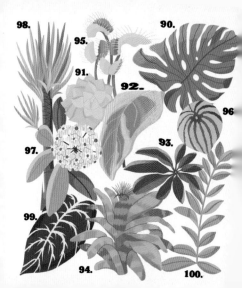

96/ WATERMELON PEPEROMIA
Peperomia argyreia

This plant's leaves may resemble the rind of a watermelon, with an unusual mix of green and silvery stripes, but it bears no actual relation to the fruit itself. A South American native, this plant can flower, but its flowers are considered unremarkable—it's really all about those stunning leaves. This is a great plant for beginners, requiring minimal care.

97/ WAX PLANT
Hoya carnosa

As the name promises, this plant's bright-green leaves have a distinctive waxy texture. They tumble over the edge of planters in thick, ropy vines; with sufficient light, it may even bloom with sweet-smelling pink and red star-shaped flowers with a porcelain-like texture. It may look like a succulent, but it's not, so don't forget to water this plant.

98/ YUCCA
Yucca gigantea

The yucca genus includes more than 40 perennial plants, but just a few are grown as houseplants. One is *Yucca gigantea*, which almost looks like a mini palm tree with a thin trunk topped with a profusion of long, slender green leaves with pointed tips. It will eventually grow out of most indoor spaces, but that will take years.

99/ ZEBRA PLANT
Aphelandra squarrosa

Bright-white veins on large dark-green leaves give this plant a distinctive zebra-stripe look. It becomes even more stunning in the early autumn when it blooms with otherworldly, pineapple-colored flowers that span several inches and last a month or more. But be forewarned: This slow-growing plant can be temperamental and needs bright, indirect light, warmth, and humidity.